M

D1180397

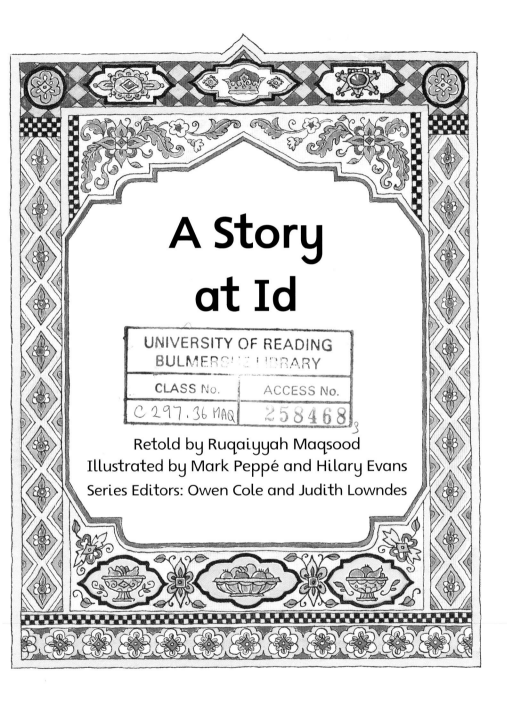

A Story
at Id

Retold by Ruqaiyyah Maqsood
Illustrated by Mark Peppé and Hilary Evans
Series Editors: Owen Cole and Judith Lowndes

Series Editors: Owen Cole and Judith Lowndes
Grateful thanks to E H Bladon for advice on the story and its
representation.

Heinemann Educational Publishers
Halley Court, Jordan Hill, Oxford OX2 8EJ

MADRID   ATHENS   PARIS
FLORENCE   PRAGUE   WARSAW
PORTSMOUTH NH   CHICAGO   SAO PAULO
SINGAPORE   TOKYO   MELBOURNE   AUCKLAND
IBADAN   GABORONE   JOHANNESBURG

First published 1995

95 96 97 98 99 10 9 8 7 6 5 4 3 2 1

British Library Cataloguing in Publication Data
A catalogue record for this book is available from the British Library

Starter Pack
1 of each of 12 titles: ISBN 0 435 01066 2

Library Hardback Edition
A Story at Id: ISBN 0 431 07755 X
1 of each of 12 titles: ISBN 0 431 07763 0

Designed by Sue Vaudin; printed and bound in Hong Kong

Acknowledgements
Back cover photograph: Mosque in Regent's Park,
Carlos Reyes-Manzo, Andes Press Agency

In this story the author has used the word *God* to aid readability for young readers.
Muslims often use the Arabic word *Allah* for God since they feel it better represents
God's indivisibility.
Pronunciation: The final 'i' in Ibrahim is a long vowel, as in 'seem', the 'dh' in Adha
is like the 'th' in 'that'.

These children are Muslims.

Every year Muslims enjoy a happy
time called Id-ul-Adha.

The children are very excited.

The children have a special
bath the night before Id.
On Id morning they get up very very early.
They put on brand new clothes.

Then they go to the mosque to pray.
There are hundreds of people going
to the mosque.
All their friends are going too.

They think about God's love and kindness.
They remember that sometimes people
have to face tests.
They remember the story of Ibrahim.

Ibrahim lived hundreds of years ago.

He was a great leader.

He had to face a test.

The Story of Ibrahim

One day God spoke to
Ibrahim.
After that day Ibrahim
spent all his life
working for God.
He showed people how to
please God.

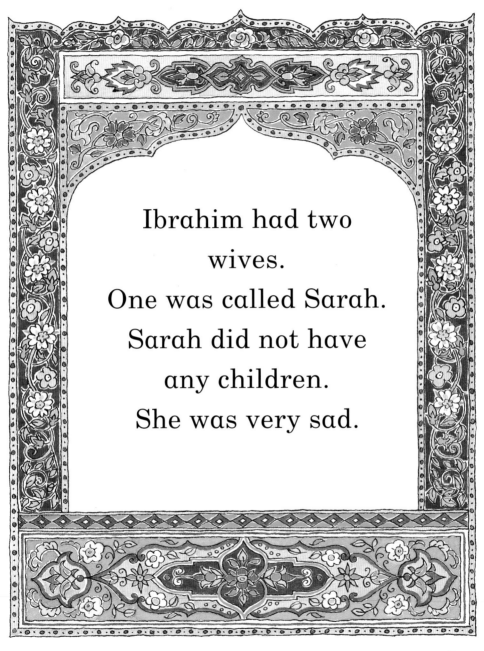

Ibrahim had two
wives.
One was called Sarah.
Sarah did not have
any children.
She was very sad.

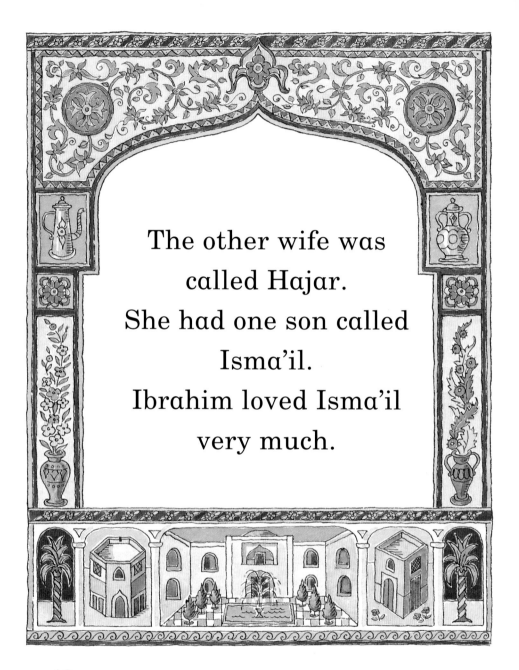

The other wife was
called Hajar.
She had one son called
Isma'il.
Ibrahim loved Isma'il
very much.

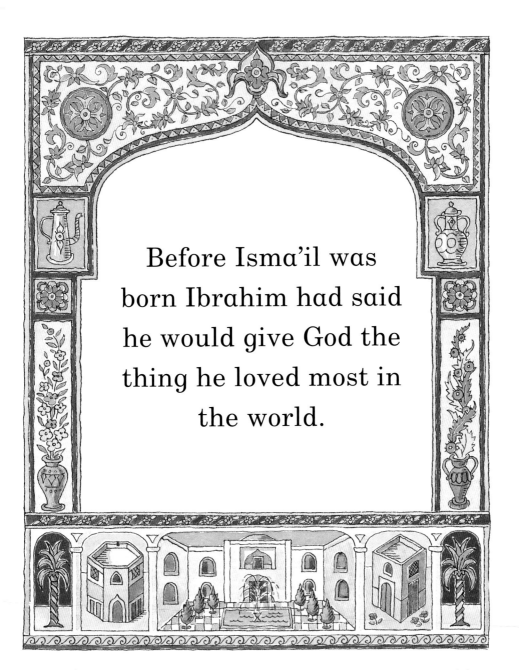

Before Isma'il was
born Ibrahim had said
he would give God the
thing he loved most in
the world.

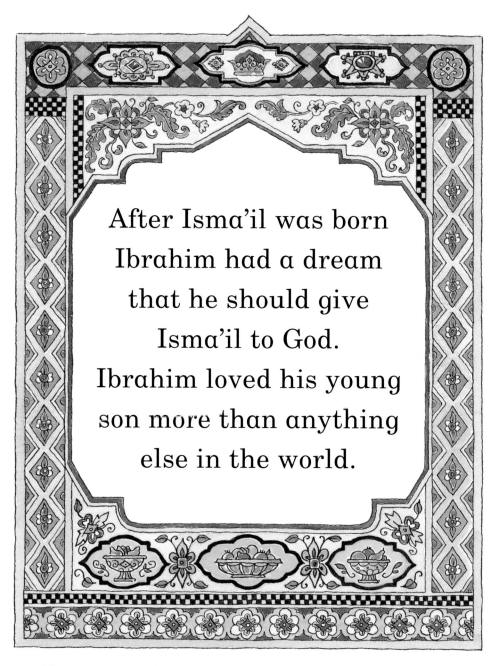

After Isma'il was born
Ibrahim had a dream
that he should give
Isma'il to God.
Ibrahim loved his young
son more than anything
else in the world.

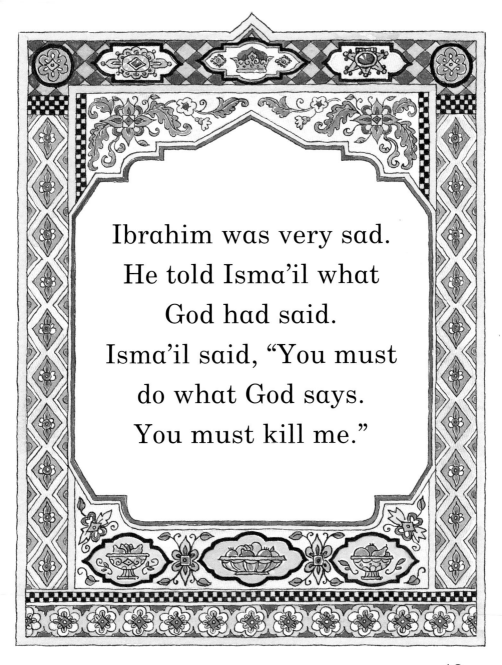

Ibrahim was very sad.
He told Isma'il what
God had said.
Isma'il said, "You must
do what God says.
You must kill me."

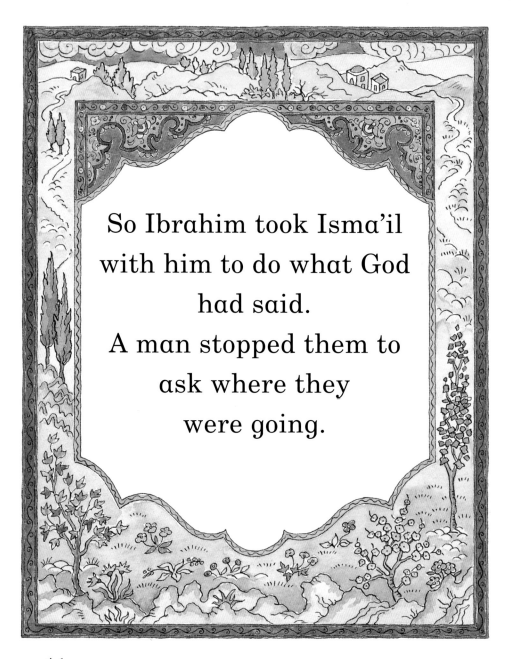

So Ibrahim took Isma'il
with him to do what God
had said.
A man stopped them to
ask where they
were going.

Ibrahim told him what
God had said.
The man said, "God did
not tell you to kill
your son.
Let him live."
Ibrahim did not listen.

Then the man spoke to
Isma'il.
"Your father wants to
kill you," said the
stranger.
"You must run away!"
Isma'il did not listen.

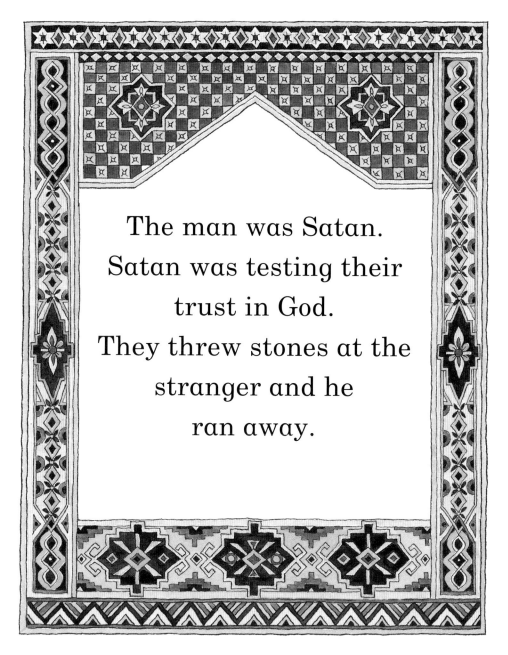

The man was Satan.
Satan was testing their
trust in God.
They threw stones at the
stranger and he
ran away.

Ibrahim knew it was
time to kill his son.
Isma'il did not run away.
Ibrahim raised his knife.

Suddenly they
heard a voice.
"Do not kill your son,
Ibrahim," said the voice.
"You have proved your
trust and love."

Isma'il did not
need to die.
As a reward, Ibrahim's
sad wife Sarah had a
baby too.

Muslims remember this story at Id-ul-Adha.
After the prayer everybody hugs and
kisses and says "Id Mubarak" which
means "Happy Feast Day".

The children get money and
sweets, presents and cards.

On Id Day, the family pays for a whole
sheep and shares the meat with other
people who are poor.

The day ends with a big party for
all the family.
Poor and lonely people are invited too.
Everyone is happy.